RIVER'S
EDGE

RIVER'S EDGE

Owen Bullock

RECENT WORK PRESS

River's Edge
Recent Work Press
Canberra, Australia

Copyright © Owen Bullock 2016

National Library of Australia
Cataloguing-in-Publication entry.

Bullock, Owen

River's Edge/ Owen Bullock

ISBN:9780994456526 (paperback)

NZ821.3

All rights reserved. This book is copyright. Except for private study, research, criticism or reviews as permitted under the Copyright Act, no part of this book may be reproduced, stored in a retrieval system, or transmitted in any form by any means without prior written permission. Enquiries should be addressed to the publisher.

Cover design: Recent Work Press
Set in Bembo by Recent Work Press

recentworkpress.com

This book is dedicated to

Brian Mark Bullock (1963-2013)

and

Martin Lucas (1962-2014)

A few years ago, I found myself without sufficient editing and teaching work to sustain a living. I chose to do some care-giving though, of course, it was badly paid. I'd tried nursing as a young man, mostly working in hospitals where I found the daily routine crushing and the lack of quality time with patients a frustration. This time I was visiting elderly people in their own homes, which was far more meaningful. They told stories in which their wisdom shone through. Many of these haiku concern such visits. Others celebrate the beach and the river and honour mentors, both living and passing.

dusting

her little vases

this is my devotion

his voice younger

as he talks about

his wife

on the piano

photos of the ones

who don't visit

nodding to her story

as if

for the first time

a scrap of paper

with the word 'love' on it

down the garbage disposal

this storm

blows sand

along sand

silence

after the wave breaks

silence

a gap

then the rainbow touches

another cloud

the blush

in the sky has faded

morning

a blue butterfly

on a dandelion . . .

you're free of burdens now

a leaf

slowly to earth

hindered by a cobweb

for Brian

to the end of the drive

with his walker

the ocean's still there, he says

hopeless thoughts . . .

seaweed

around my ankles

he reaches his chair

with more courage

than any Olympian

corridor

the nurse's hair

follows the nurse

a little boy

looking back and back

at the man in the wheelchair

eleven months old

all the adults

start crawling again

thinking of your hands

on the building site

classical guitarist

home for a while

she sorts shells

in the sand

in the surf

a skinhead

breast-stroking

old notebook

his daughter's

recipe

dreams of Cornwall

so vivid

I want to pay my rates

walking a road

I drive daily

nothing familiar

fence wire

oscillating blue

the water drop

mid-spring

my mentor rings me

for advice

river crossing

beware the smoothest

stones

shopping for clothes

wanting to buy

what I'm wearing

suddenly

in the café

no one is talking

stillness after rain

a river

of sky

unable to remember

what was in the dream

what was in life

getting younger

each day that passes

river's edge

for Caron

emptiness

of the room

first light

lit drop

of condensation

almost blinding

early start

snowdrops

see me off

back to work

vacuuming

Christmas stars

New Year's Eve

to New Year's Day

the unlit candle

old clocks

that don't work

top his kitchen cupboards

as he's talking

I study

his teeth

massaging

my male client's back

in a bloke-ish way

scrawled on a scrap

a tip for the 6.30

Black Romeo

not good news . . .

he puts the lid back

on the jam

spectral light

the photo of his son

who died young

in his bedroom

seven pictures

of his Saviour

stepping back

cherry petals

on the abandoned farm

cemetery

the age old problem

of finding the dead

if I don't

pick this flower it has

a few days more

watering

the zen garden

with water

meditation

I let go

what I lost

somewhere

in that mass of cloud

a few of your cells

to the far shore

my mentor

is travelling

for Martin

ahead the pouring light

fishermen . . .

I look at the place

that they left

some of the waves

overtaking

the others

old house bus

indicates left

goes right

avoiding the bumps mascara in progress

after making love

saying what I wanted to say

before

I can't take

my eyes off you

another breakfast

the old farmer

his winter day in town

short shorts

downpour

a fisherman smokes a cigarette

beneath his hat

shadow of a cross

on the speed sign

winter afternoon

cluck rasp laugh the tui is home

winter light –

how long have I been driving

in the wrong gear?

from his taxi

the loneliness

of night

taxi cab

the clock

clicks

for John O'Connor

dusk

birdsong pulls you

closer

the wake of the scaup

keeps widening . . .

my love for you

for Sue

white rose petals

fall to the hearth

quiet autumn night

winds

through the chimney

an ancient proverb

wave lift

phosphorescent

moonlight

black swan

water drops

jewel the neck

Acknowledgements:

Kokako, When North Meets South (NZ); *bottle rockets, Cattails, Frogpond, The Heron's Nest, The Sacred in Contemporary Haiku* and *Beyond the Grave: Contemporary Afterlife Haiku* ed. Robert Epstein (US); *Evening Breeze – Janice M Bostok Haiku Award Anthology 2012, paper wasp* (Australia); *The Cornish Banner/ An Baner Kernewek, Presence, Notes From the Gean* (UK); *Sharpening the Green Pencil 2013* (Romania); *Vladimir Devidé Haiku Award – Selected Haiku 2013, 5th Yamadera Basho Memorial Museum Contest – Selected Haiku 2013* (Japan); *A Hundred Gourds, World Haiku Review* (International).

'on the piano', Highly Commended, Irish Haiku Association Competition, 2012

'a little boy', Runner-Up, Vladimir Devidé Haiku Award, 2013

'stepping back', Honourable Mention, Vancouver Cherry Blossom Festival 2013 Haiku Invitational

'avoiding the bumps', Commended, Kokako Haiku Competition, 2013

'black swan', Co-Winner, 17th Haiku International Association Contest, 2015

Thanks to Sue Peachey and Shane Strange.

This is Owen Bullock's fourth collection of haiku, following *urban haiku* (Recent Work Press, 2015), *breakfast with epiphanies* (Oceanbooks, NZ, 2012) and *wild camomile* (Post Pressed, Australia, 2009). He has also published a collection of poetry, *sometimes the sky isn't big enough* (Steele Roberts, NZ, 2010); the novella, *A Cornish Story* (Palores, UK, 2010), and a number of chapbooks of haiku and poetry. Owen is a former editor of *Kokako*, New Zealand's only specialist haiku magazine, and has edited numerous other journals and anthologies, including *Poetry New Zealand*. He is a PhD Candidate at the University of Canberra. Last year, he won the Canberra Critics' Circle Award for Poetry.

"*urban haiku* continues to reward re-reading, while reminding us that Owen Bullock – an experienced, confident, experimental practitioner in Japanese-based poetic forms – is every bit as much a student of humanity...as he is of haiku."
- Rodney Williams, *One Hundred Gourds*

available from
recentworkpress.com